Summary Bun Ideation | R

Publishing: Inc̲̲̲̲̲̲ Summary of Let Trump Be Trump & Summary of Made to Stick

By:

Corey R Lewandowski

& David N Bossie

Proudly Brought to you by:

READTREPRENEUR
—— WORLD'S BEST BOOK SUMMARIES ——

Text Copyright © Readtrepreneur

Legal & Disclaimer

damages or injury caused by the use and application, whether directly or indirectly, of any advice or information presented, whether for breach of contract, tort, negligence, personal injury, criminal intent, or under any other cause of action.

You agree to accept all risks of using the information presented inside this book. You need to consult a professional medical practitioner in order to ensure you are both able and healthy enough to participate in this program.

Table of Contents

The Book at a Glance

Donald J. Trump's victory would be the most unconventional victory in U.S. presidential election history. The brain trust of the Republican party not only believed that Trump had no chance to win against Hillary Clinton, but many of them actually lobbied Trump not to run, and opposed his nomination up to the very day that he won it.

The book is the gripping inside story of the Trump campaign as told from the standpoint of two campaign managers who were ensconced deep in the day-to-day operations of Team Trump.

As most anthologies of successful campaigns go, the first part describes the end result of what is always a grueling process: the victory and celebration of the candidate. Chapter 1 begins with the end, as Donald Trump makes his successful march to the podium at the New York Hilton to deliver his acceptance speech as the 45th president of the United States.

David Bossie was born in Boston, Massachussets, and was the Deputy Campaign Manager of Trump presidential campaign. He attended Towson State University and the University of Maryland, but left college to help in the campaigns of Ronald Reagan and Bob Dole. He has been the

President and Chairman since 2000. He is married to Susan Bossie and has four children. He lives in Maryland.

Corey R. Lewandowski was the first full-time manager of the Trump campaign, and was responsible for setting up the original campaign team from scratch. He assembled the campaign framework from which Trump won the Republican presidential primary. He was born and raised in Lowell, Massachusetts, and graduated with a B.A. in Political Science from the University of Massachusetts at Lowell, and a Masters from the American University in Washington, DC. He has been involved in politics even before graduating from college, and has been on campaign of various Republican candidates for over twenty years. He has recently worked as a lobbyist, and has appeared as a political commentator in various cable and network stations. He is married to Alison Hardy and has four children. He lives in New Hampshire.

Chapter 1 - ELECTION NIGHT

The chapter is aptly prefaced with quotes from three mainstream media sources who opine that Trump had no chance in winning the 2016 presidential elections. Everyone knows of course, that the elections ended with Donald J. Trump delivering a victory speech at the New York Hilton on what was effectively the morning after election night, November 9th, 2016.

The day of the election did not begin well for Trump and his campaign staff. In the afternoon, author Dave Bossie was coming back from an interview with Halle Jackson of MSNBC asking him where he thought the Trump campaign was going. With a lot of uncertainty less than eight hours before the polls closed, Trump's children, Don Jr., Ivanka, Don Jr.'s wife, Vanessa, Eric, and Eric's wife, Lara, were feverishly working the phones ginning up support for their father.

At the Republican National Headquarters, the mood was not upbeat. Its data team calculated that Donald Trump would only get 204 of the 270 electoral votes needed to win the presidency. Their analysis was showing that Trump would probably not win any of the battleground states, and even lose a few that had gone solidly Republican in the past few elections. Even Sean Spicer, who would be Trump's first presidential spokesman, was already talking to the television and cable networks about jobs as a political analyst. Spicer and Katie Walsh, the RNC's chief of staff, instead wanted to talk about certain senatorial and congressional races, instead of the race at the top of the ticket.

At 5 p.m., things were going into panic mode in the Trump campaign. Former Trump campaign staffer Corey R. Lewandowski was in CNN headquarters having to listen to prognostications by mainstream media talking heads like Jake Tapper, John King, and Wolf Blitzer. Reporters like them publicly professed their objectivity about the race results, but the real truth is that almost to a man, they wanted Trump to lose the elections. Just minutes later, ABC senior producer Chris Vlasto calls up Dave Bossie and tells him that the exit polling is showing Trump is down from anywhere between 5-8 points in eight of the declared battleground states, a situation that no presidential candidate before Trump had ever come back from.

Bossie convenes Trump campaign CEO Steve Bannon, Trump's son-in-law Jared Kushner, and RNC chairman Lance Priebus, and tell them the sobering news. Kushner then gets on the phone with Melania, Trump's wife, with the gloomy assessment. Melania informs Trump of the news, and he responds by saying that this was all "a waste of time and money". While the numbers look bad on the surface, Bossie sees some minor inconsistencies in the exit polling numbers and believes that the gloomy assessment may be a little premature.

A few minutes later, the campaign brain trust, Trump, his family, together with vice-presidential running mate Mike Pence and his family, convene in the 14th floor of the Trump Towers to watch the election returns come in. Joining them are former Republican party presidential nomination rivals Dr. Ben Carson, and New Jersey Governor Chris Christie, together with Bob Mercer, a reclusive billionaire supporter. It was time to let things go. All the hard campaign work had been done, and it was simply just a matter of time to see what fate had in store.

As it turns out, Bossie's assessment of the preliminary numbers were correct. The exit polls were in fact, skewed towards the Democratic candidate. Around 11 p.m., Trump begins picking off one battleground state after another, until the Associated Press has no choice but to call the elections for Donald J. Trump in the wee hours of November 9th, 2016. A gracious concession phone call from Hillary Clinton and a Trump victory acceptance speech would seal the night's success as the country had its 45th President.

Chapter 2 - HOUSE MONEY

Donald Trump, it turns out, is a superstitious man. He believes that little rituals give him good luck. While he has always said publicly that you make your own luck, he still follows rituals that many believe account for his success in his ventures in television, publishing, hotels, real estate, and after November 8th, politics.

Speaking of luck, it was incidentally in Las Vegas where Dave Bossie first got into contact with Donald Trump. Sometime in 2010, Bossie was in Las Vegas soliciting for sponsors for a golf tournament to benefit a charity for the Children's National Medical Center in Washington, D.C. David's son, Griffin, fought for his life in the hospital, where doctors worked hard to fix holes in the little boy's heart and saved him.

In Vegas, Bossie meets with Steve Wynn, billionaire owner of Wynn hotels and casinos in Las Vegas and Macau, who pledges valuable prizes for the golf tournament that Bossie is organizing. Bossie knows that Wynn is a close friend of another billionaire, Donald Trump, a known golf aficionado. He asks Wynn if he can introduce him to Trump - Wynn obliges and immediately hooks up Bossie on a telephone call to Trump, who promises that he would be glad to help with the golf tournament.

Formally introduced, Bossie finds himself on the elevator

towards the magnificent 26th floor offices of Donald Trump at the Trump Tower in New York City just two weeks later. He has a laundry list of items that he would be asking Trump, aside from asking him to host the tournament in his golf course. Full of nerves prior to meeting "The Donald", Bossie is quickly calmed down when Trump turns out to be a gracious and engaging host. Trump not only agrees to provide all the items that he asked for, Trump throws in a $5,000 donation to the Children's National Medical Center.

Bossie would talk to Trump many times over the next year. However, Trump would give Bossie a pivotal call in 2011, when in June of that year, Mitt Romney announced that he was throwing in his hat into the presidential race in 2012 as the Republican candidate. Acknowledging privately that Romney would be a "terrible candidate", Trump commissions Bossie to conduct a poll to test the waters for a Trump presidential run. The poll that Bossie conducts shows that while Trump certainly has name recognition and other positives, an overwhelming majority of people believe that he will not run anyway, a fatal negative. Trump does not run and instead throws in his support for Romney, endorsing him on January 2nd, 2012. Romney loses decisively to Barack Obama in November of that year.

Chapter 3 - NEW HAMPSHIRE

Many people say that only egomaniacs and crazy people would want to run for president of the United States. It is an emotional, mental, and physical gauntlet that requires a lot of time, travel, and a bucket load of money, 99% of which they will have to ask, wheedle, cajole, and beg for. When the press got wind of Trump's intention to jump into the race, they were still suspicious and cynical: "It's all ego-driven", "He's just building his brand", and "He's got a new TV deal".

While ego has always been ascribed to Trump, it was never a factor in his decision to run. While driving in New York one night with Keith Schiller, his bodyguard since 1999, and one of his longest serving employees, they observed that throngs of people would paw at Trump as he was walking around New York City inspecting his properties. Pondering whether to announce his bid to run for president, he tells Schiller that it was a big thing to run for U.S. President, that it was indeed "big shit". He tells Schiller, "You and me, Keith, we're hotter than we've ever been, yep, you and me".

By 2013, now seriously considering running for the presidency in 2016, Trump began to lay the groundwork. He hired a young political operative, Sam Nunberg, a lawyer who was helping Trump navigate the political landscape, while also assisting him with political speeches and scheduling. Trump would, however, increase the frequency of his phone calls to Bossie, who was increasingly becoming a reliable political resource. On Bossie's urging, Trump would ramp up his Republican credentials that year. He gives a speech to open the second day at the Conservative Political Action Conference (CPAC), accompanied by Bossie. While his speech did not generate the requisite electricity, he had at least stamped his presence as a serious candidate. He also aligns his party politics with his campaign contributions, shutting off his support to Democratic candidates and giving the maximum allowed money to Republican candidates. He is also introduced to the major lights in the Republican party at the time, such as the former U.S. Senator from Pennsylvania, Rick Santorum, himself a former presidential candidate.

In the meantime, Bossie gets busy arranging for a Freedom Summit and enlists Republican luminaries such as Senators Ted Cruz (Texas), Rand Paul (Kentucky), and former Speaker Newt Gingrich, among others. While Paul and Cruz were the stars and gave rousing speeches, Trump, the political outsider and newcomer, stole the show. It was during this time that Trump uttered his groundbreaking campaign slogan for the first time: "We have to make America great again". This moment was to presage his impending assault on the status quo that he felt had left America stagnant. From this moment, no institution of the ruling would be safe: not the government, nor the Catholic Church, the media, or even his own Republican party.

Despite his performance in this event, mainstream media reporters still kept away from Trump, thinking that he was a flash in the pan. Not so with Steve Bannon, however. Bannon was the conservative firebrand who was hosting the *Breitbart* show on Sirius XM radio. Bossie approached Bannon and asked him if he wanted to meet Donald Trump while he made a presentation regarding a possible presidential campaign. Bannon accompanied Bossie for the meeting where Bossie laid out what a presidential campaign entailed in terms of manpower, logistics, and of course, cost. Trump impressed both men with his ability to pick up things quickly, but Bannon told Bossie that Trump's chances in the presidential election were "less than zero".

Despite the daunting time, effort, and resources that would be required to run for president, Trump appeared to be serious about throwing his hat in the ring. In 2014, he asked David to look for a manager to run his campaign. Bossie had lots of names in mind because of his wide network, but there were two major considerations, if not roadblocks, in getting someone to work for Trump. First, the person would actually have to believe that Trump was really running for president. Second, and more challenging, he needed to find someone who had the temperament and personality to work with Trump. Trump, as everyone knew by then, is an abrasive taskmaster who likes to call the shots. He would not be a traditional candidate in a non-traditional campaign, so Bossie needed to look for a non-traditional political handler.

This is when Corey R. Lewandowski came to mind. Lewandowski was a proven political operative who had had almost twenty years of experience in practically every aspect of political campaigning. Bossie felt that with Corey R. Lewandowski's all-around experience, his toughness, and having dealt with all sorts of candidates, he would be the perfect campaign manager for Trump. On October 14th, 2014, Lewandowski agrees to at least meet Trump.

Chapter 4 - YOU'RE HIRED

Donald Trump valued two things more than anything in people that worked for him: loyalty and work ethic. Any campaign manager or staffer who wanted to work for him needed the two qualities in spades. When Corey R. Lewandowski met Trump for the first time in his offices in the twenty-sixth in the Trump Towers, he was taken aback by what comprised the Trump campaign operation at that point: a young attorney named Sam Nunberg, a desk, and the candidate.

Lewandowski then notices that Trump reads voraciously and takes his mail very seriously, going through each one on a daily basis. Trump tells Lewandowski that he owns several aircrafts, houses, and golf courses, things that Lewandowski would have known about anyway. He then tells Trump that the cost to campaign in the first three primaries will cost $25 million. He also warns Trump that he will spend the money as it were his own, and that he believes that Trump's chances of winning are at 5%. Trump responds that he believes his chances stand at 10%, not 5%, and to that point seems undaunted by the potential cost, which will come from his pocket, and the terrible odds. Trump then asks him what he wants to get paid. Lewandowski responds with $20,000 and there is very little negotiating from the man who wrote a book on negotiation. Corey R. Lewandowski is hired on the spot as Trump's first official campaign manager.

Chapter 5 - THE ISLAND OF THE MISFIT TOYS

The mainstream media, who were against the Donald Trump candidacy from the beginning, shared an assessment that Donald Trump's campaign was a disorganized mess. Absent from Trump's campaign was the army of expensive career politicos who were supposed to know all the nuances of an effective campaign. Trump, the quintessential businessman, wanted his personal stamp on the campaign operations, and spending wasn't a matter of spending a lot or spending too little, but rather, spending wisely. He chose people whom he trusted and who had the same outlook. Despite the outward frugality, he never turned down a spending request.

Lewandowski took on his job when there was not even a skeleton of a campaign operation. The toughest challenge was that he had to acclimatize himself to the personal habits of his boss. Trump managed most of his affairs by phone, but allowed time to meet with Corey twice a day. As he was getting used to his surroundings in the Trump Towers, he was also putting together a campaign plan with a small skeleton crew and a tiny office. This situation would not last very long. Presidential campaign teams become as large as army battalions before it is all over.

His first hires were managers for each of the first three

caucus states. He made sure he hired people who knew the districts and voters of the three states very well. They were all experienced political operatives who would be operating in those states, and report back to the New York home base in the Trump Towers.

For South Carolina, he hired Jim Merrill, who owned a marketing and public relations company in the state. Merrill was also a member of the South Carolina House of Representatives since 2000, where he was the majority leader. He also hired Ed McMullen, a businessman who was involved in South Carolina politics for twenty-five years. He was also a former president of a conservative think tank, the South Carolina Policy Council. Finally, he also hired Geri McDaniel, another experienced political operative, for the South Carolina effort.

For New Hampshire, he hired Matt Cipielowski, a local boy who knew New Hampshire politics in and out, and was Lewandowski's field director at Americans for Prosperity.

Finally, he hired Chuck Laudner for Iowa. Laudner was the former chief of staff of Congressman Steve King, and had been the executive director of the Iowa Republican Party. His Iowa credentials were solidified when he helped Rick Santorum win the Iowa caucus in 2012.

Early in 2015, Trump had his first taste of caucus

campaigning when he flew to Iowa to speak in front of plain folk – Iowa farmers in a Des Moines agricultural conference called the Land Investment Expo. The campaign staff was confident that Trump was a wonderful communicator who could connect with all sorts of people from all economic classes no matter what city or state they were from. After the Expo, they attended a dinner for state Republicans where Trump gave the first broad outlines of what would be his major policy initiatives. These would eventually draw voters, as well as intense criticism from opponents and the mainstream media: keeping jobs in America, trade, Chinese relations, and of course, border fences.

Laudner, who had seen it all in Iowa politics, made a prescient comment after the dinner: Trump would win the Iowa caucus, which was still over a year away.

The next day, Bossie's Citizens United hosted the Iowa Freedom Summit at the Hoyt Sherman Place, a 1,500-seat historic theater complete with a raised proscenium stage. The twelve Republican presidential candidates went on stage to be presented for the first time in a caucus campaign event. Trump gave a speech that the *Des Moines Register* editorialized as "brazen", that the newspaper ranked a distant second to the speech that Wisconsin governor, Scott Walker had delivered. The next day, people had forgotten all about

Walker.

With a shortage of office space, Lewandowski could not expand his campaign staff significantly because of the tiny quarters they had in the Trump Towers. All he could do was to hire a few interns, including a lawyer-friend from Kansas, Alan Cobb, who worked on Bob Dole's campaign years earlier. Now Lewandowski also had to assemble a core team.

His first hires were people that had no political experience, but had extensive knowledge of Trump and his organization. He started with Dan Scavino, who worked at the Briar Hall Country Club in Westchester, New York, as Trump's regular caddy. He had been moving up the Trump organization and was on his way to starting up a PR firm before being convinced to join the campaign. He would become Trump's Twitter lieutenant.

He also hired Hope Hicks, a young looker who handled PR work for Trump's golf tournaments. She would handle PR for the first stages of the Trump campaign. The retired New York PD policeman, Keith Schiller, came on board as the chief of campaign security, together with a small crew of former FBI agents.

Another political neophyte was a former quarterback from the University of Connecticut, John McEntee, who turned out to be hardest working staffer on the Trump campaign team. McEntee became an important member of the advance team, who flew to campaign stops to prep the Trump campaign team beforehand.

Lewandowski then asked a partner at Jones Day, Don McGahn, whose most important credential was that he was a former chairman of the Federal Election Commission, and was a campaign finance law expert. Lewandowski also convinced former Tea Party spokesperson Katrina Pierson to come on board as the campaign's first national campaign spokesperson.

Pierson and McGahn were one of the very few people who were involved in politics that joined Trump's initial campaign team, but their enthusiasm and loyalty for Trump was unquestioned.

The next big event for Trump was CPAC, which was held in late February 2015, and as they were planning for it, Lewandowski found a bigger space for offices in the fifth floor of the Trump Towers. The space took up half the floor.

The initial set up was complete. The first campaign staff had no so-called "chief strategist", speechwriter, pollsters, or "professional political consultants" that that were all over the place for the past eight years in the Republican party's unsuccessful bids to help elect a president. What they had was an island of misfit toys.

Chapter 6 - THE GOLDEN ESCALATOR

Donald J. Trump, despite charges that he has flip-flopped on some policy issues, has been consistent on one thing: putting America first. He said so when he first appeared on the *Oprah Winfrey Show* in 1988 and he carried this theme all the way to his presidential campaign. Trump was a hard worker who probably put in more hours than anyone who worked for him. This is why he was sometimes called the "Blue Collar Millionaire".

Early in 2015, with the semblance of a campaign staff in place and a handful of political appearances under his belt, the only thing left to do was to make a formal announcement of his intention to run for president. Even while enjoying a well-deserved vacation in Aruba with his family in May of 2015, Lewandowski was taking ten phone calls from Trump every day to talk about campaign details.

One morning, Lewandowski takes a phone call from Michael Cohen, Trump's attorney, who says that Trump would like to make an announcement in late May. Lewandowski says that this is impossible because it takes a minimum of five weeks to plan the event. Lewandowski also provided Cohen with a rundown of what days were best for the announcement, and why some days were a no-no, such as Mondays and Fridays.

After some back and forth, they finally agreed on a day, June 16th, 2015, to make the announcement. While having breakfast with his family the next day, Lewandowski gets a call from Trump, who asks him where he was. Even after saying he was in Aruba, Trump tells him to "get your ass back here".

In preparation for the big event, Trump was baiting the media running towards the announcement date. He said he was going to make an announcement on June 16th, without actually telling what it was going to be. Many in the mainstream media, as well as pundits, were convinced that as in years before, Trump would never formally run for president. Besides, they all felt that he didn't have any chance of even getting the Republican nomination.

As the date was approaching, he was beginning to float policy balloons. In his keeping with his America First motto, he criticized the Trans-Pacific Partnership trade pact that he felt would be a disaster for the United States. Many pundits believed that Trump got his policy ideas from prodding from insiders like Steve Bannon. However, Bannon himself denied this. Trump was actually using interviews, and there were many, from media types to understand how his policy messages were resonating with the public.

When the day for the big announcement came, they decided that the announcement would be made at the Trump Towers. Leading up to the announcement, Lewandowski had to deal with various personalities in and out of the Trump universe. There was the chief operating officer of Trump Properties, Matt Calamari, who was first spotted by Trump when he was a security guard at the U.S. Open Tennis Tournament in Queens, New York.

Calamari had worked for Trump for 35 years. The intimidating Calamari treated the Trump Tower as if he owned it. Lewandowski also introduced his own campaign event "expert", George Gigicos, a staging expert who had worked for President George W. Bush, Mitt Romney, and John McCain. While Trump did not take quickly to Gigicos, Gigico's efficiency and effectiveness eventually won over Trump, and gained that most important commodity with the Boss, trust. He ended up heading the advance team for the campaign. It was this trust that Trump bestowed on Lewandowski when Trump asked him to stay in one of his lavish gold-plated apartments in New York City when Trump found that he was having a hard time looking for a place to stay in leading up to the announcement.

At the announcement, Trump uttered the words that would throw him into the fire of the campaign's first serious controversy. In about thirty words, he said something to the effect that Mexico was sending over people to the United States that has lots of "problems". Trump said that they were rapists who also brought crime and drugs. He added, however, that, "some, I assume, are good people".

Before they kicked off their third campaign stop in South Carolina, Dylann Roof, a racist from the state, walked into a historic black church in downtown Charleston, shot and killed nine people who were attending church service. Because of this event, Trump ordered the campaign to cancel all their trips to South Carolina in deference to the horrific shooting.

Trump's campaign took a major shot in the bow when the Democrat candidate, Hillary Clinton, put some of the blame on the shooting on Trump, referencing his statement about the Mexicans during his announcement. She suggested that the comments made by Trump tended to "trigger" unstable people into committing heinous acts.

Clinton, with the assistance of the mainstream media, succeeded in creating a hubbub that prompted knee-jerk responses from many: Neil Young, who used to be a friend, informed the Trump campaign that it could no longer use his music. NBC then "fired" him from *The Apprentice*, Macy's dumped the Trump clothing line, and the Trump-owned *Miss Universe* pageant began to bleed sponsors.

The blowback had an unintended effect that the mainstream media and Clinton did not anticipate: her comment opened the eyes of a multitude of Republicans who were not turned on the idea of voting for Trump. More importantly, it inflamed the ones who already wanted to vote for Trump to do more.

The mainstream media thought they had delivered a knockout punch, and thought that Trump would back-track from his comments. In a phone interview with CNN's anchor Don Lemon, a supposedly "objective" reporter who had not hidden his disgust from Trump, Lemon asks Trump if he would take back his comments. Trump responds by saying that, "somebody has to do the raping".

Chapter 7 - UP IN THE AIR

The mainstream media pounced on every politically incorrect statement that Trump made, trying to inflame voters against him, especially announcements that he made regarding immigration and border protection. They believed and hoped that every politically charged statement that he made would be a mortal blow to his campaign.

The media also sought to downplay the responses that he received in public appearances. This was the case, for example, in Laredo, Texas, where he met with local officials and border patrol officers. To bolster his border protection credentials, Trump spent a lot of time campaigning among border enforcement police in border states like Arizona and Texas. In Laredo, he got a warm reception from local officials, including the Democrat mayor, and border patrol police. The media did not report on this enthusiastic welcome, but instead reported on protests that were being made based on lies that the media had reported on the thirty something words that he uttered regarding Mexicans.

Trump also started having issues with women. Moderating the debates among the Republican candidates, *Fox News* anchor Megyn Kelly sandbagged Trump, and pinned him on his inappropriate comments about women throughout his life.

Trump clawed back hard at Kelly, criticizing her, and saying that he would have nothing to do with her again. His comments about comedienne Rosie O'Donnell being fat and ugly added to the fire. The mainstream media excoriated him for his comments, and while many figured that these events would be devastating to the campaign, it energized his supporters even more.

Part of the Trump campaign mystique was travelling on his lavishly appointed 757 jumbo jet that he used to go from one campaign stop to another. It was first class times ten when it came to Trump's planes, but when it came to food, it was down to Diet Coke, Pizza Hut, Kentucky Fried Chicken, and McDonald's. There were also the Oreos that had to be served to Trump in unopened packages, and the McDonald's milkshakes that he rewarded himself after a particularly successful campaign stop. Alluding to his New York boyhood, he called the milkshakes "malteds". Trump also liked Elton John music pumped up to maximum volume at certain times.

These were the unusual trappings for a man who took at the most, three-minute naps during campaign travel. The longest period of sleep that he was observed to have taken in a plane was thirty minutes. He was the hardest working person that the authors ever came across, and those working around him had to be as alive and awake as he was.

These were all invisible to everyone outside the campaign. Enemies saw him as a distasteful egotist, while supporters saw a man hell-bent on returning America to greatness. The latter group propelled Trump to be the front-runner in the polls for the Republican nomination by July 2015, rising from being a single-digit performer when the campaign started.

Trump always seemed to flirt with disaster whenever his poll numbers shot up. On July 18th, 2015, in an interview with a conservative values group, he said that Senator John McCain, a former presidential candidate himself, was, in his mind, not a war hero. He dismissed McCain, much of whose senatorial career was based on trumpeting his prisoner of war struggles, as someone Trump did not consider a hero because he was captured. Trump said that, "I like people who weren't captured".

The statement raised a firestorm, with the most pointed responses coming from Republicans and conservatives, who consider military service one of the most laudable occupations that an American can have. Nevertheless, Trump would not back down from his comments, and even conservative supporter Sean Hannity of *Fox News* and Steve Bannon asked him to walk back.

Despite the Mexican and McCain comments, Trump

continued to lead in the polls, even as most analysts and the mainstream media believed that his campaign was just a sideshow that was just a neat marketing trick for his business empire.

Chapter 8 - THE DELEGATE HUNTER

With all the controversy and juicy gossip that Donald Trump constantly generated, he was, far and away, the leader in amassing what is known in the media business as "earned media". This is an industry term for free media coverage and exposure that a candidate gets through interviews, news coverage, and political and editorial coverage via television and cable. It is converted into a money equivalent, and quantifies how much a candidate would have spent if he paid for the coverage himself.

Throughout the campaign, Trump earned almost 2 billion dollars in earned media, where he got free coverage on television, radio, print media, Twitter, Reddit, and Facebook. This was more than Hillary Clinton and all the other sixteen Republican candidates COMBINED. In February 2016 alone, Trump got $400 million in earned media. To put the money issue in perspective, campaign dropout Governor John Kasich of Ohio had already spent $14 million by that time, $4 million more than Trump. February is the month before "Super Tuesday", where the biggest number of U.S. states hold primary caucuses and elections. The losing Republican presidential candidate in 2012, Mitt Romney, added to Trump's earned media just days before Super Tuesday by calling Trump a "con man". The mainstream media lapped this up, thinking it was another death blow to the Trump campaign. Despite the negativity, Trump won 7 out of the 11 states that voted, and secured 256 delegates, more than anyone among the other Republican candidates.

It would be a brutal campaign coming up to Super Tuesday in March of 2016. In eight days, Trump and his core campaign staff, including Lewandowski, would travel 8,500 miles. The campaign was a punishing test of endurance from the start of the campaign to Election Day. Trump's two pilots would have flown 370,000 miles to 203 cities in 45 states, covering 722 flight segments. Trump's plane would have used up almost a million gallons of fuel, and Lewandowski would have sat beside Trump for over 1,000 hours during his stint as campaign manager.

Trump expressed and showed his appreciation for the loyal campaign staff that endured this brutal schedule. He would call up his campaign staff's family members and apologize for having to keep their spouses and parents away for important family milestones. Corey felt the warmth and appreciation from Trump, even when his days were numbered as Trump campaign head in early 2016. The unraveling of his career as Trump's campaign manager started at Trump's Florida estate, Mar-a-Lago, and the appearance of a man named Paul Manafort, a seasoned political consultant.

Manafort was recommended to Trump by Tom Barrack, a billionaire real estate investor who was a close friend of Donald Trump. From the beginning, Lewandowski felt that he was being upstaged and being nudged aside by Manafort, whom he had confirmed as a dangerous press "leaker". Trump had brought Manafort in to be a "delegate hunter", which he believed had been Corey Lewandowski's weakness as a campaign manager. A delegate needed 1,237 delegates to win, and despite the success on Super Tuesday, Trump was still a long way's off in locking in the 1,237, and Trump felt that he needed "outside" help to do so.

Manafort was a master in manipulating people within the Trump campaign, even if he could not crack through Trump himself. He was somehow able to convince the Trump children and son-in-law Jared Kushner, that Lewandowski had many deficiencies, and after Manafort's entry, a bogus news story that Corey Lewandowski had embezzled money from the campaign. It was Don Jr. who gave Corey Lewandowski his walking papers on June 20th, 2016, barely three weeks before Donald Trump, the nominating process in the Republican national convention. Despite his firing, Corey Lewandowski refuses to make disparaging remarks about his former boss in mainstream media interviews, and has a heartfelt talk with Trump immediately after he is dumped.

Chapter 9 - THURSTON HOWELL III

Hillary Clinton and the Democrats pander to the Mexicans and immigrants – legal and illegal – because they vote overwhelmingly Democrat. Illegal aliens provide cheap labor to much of corporate America, and helps drive up profits, probably explaining why corporate America contributed more to Clinton's campaign than to Trump's. The campaign in July of 2016 was floundering with just months before the election, and the staff was plagued by intrigue and back-stabbing with Paul Manafort at the helm. Manafort had his own special circle, and kept most of the other campaign workers out of the loop, creating a cloud of mistrust and cynicism.

Right after the Republican national convention, a *New York Times* article reported that a secret meeting attended by Trump, Manafort, Ivanka, her husband Jared, former New Jersey governor Chris Christie, and communications Jason Miller. According to the report, Trump was advised to use a teleprompter, change his ways, and be "on message". Trump is enraged at this report, and after speaking with Corey Lewandowski on the phone, he is getting convinced that Manafort may be becoming a problem. When the *New York Times* publishes the article, the backlash is immediate.

Major Republican donors begin to bail, and there are talks

within the party to cut Trump loose. Republican money, they were saying, should instead go to congressional and senate races rather than to a presidential candidate that was certain to go down in flames. The conservative magazine, *The National Review*, expressed its disdain for Trump, and polling data showed that Trump was on his way to a historic defeat in the hands of Hillary Clinton. A quick fix was needed.

The fix included promoting Kellyanne Conway. Kellyanne, who was focusing on empowerment issues for women in the Trump campaign, was immediately promoted to campaign manager. After this was settled, it was time to prepare for the first debate with Hillary Clinton, scheduled for September 26th, 2016. The debate prep team would include Steve Bannon, *Fox News* head honcho Roger Ailes, Christie, and former New Mayor, Rudy Giuliani.

Just as they were starting a practice debate one morning at the Bedminster golf club, an uninvited Paul Manafort walked into the meeting dressed up like a boat captain, and looking like Thurston Howell III from Gilligan's island. Manafort's assistant, Rick Gates, had somehow found out about the meeting and informed Manafort about it. Trump dresses down Manafort immediately, asking Manafort if he thought that Trump was a baby. It would be the beginning of Manafort's quick reversal of fortunes in the 2016 presidential election cycle.

After Bannon is formally hired as a campaign staffer, he quickly enlists the services of pollsters, who up to that point, were non-existent in the campaign. It is right after this that the *New York Times*, on August 15th, ran a story that Manafort had taken a twelve-million-dollar payment from the Ukraine government. While Manafort denied this, he seemed to be doing slippery things with campaign money. Manafort had requested for over $5.7 million in funds to finance various campaign initiatives, and did not provide a proper accounting; the use of the funds never came to light.

Trump, sensing that he had a crook running his campaign, asked Bannon to fire Manafort immediately. In the end, it was Jared Kushner who took up the task of the firing. With pollsters and a new campaign team in place, it was time to go on a full-time assault against the most joyless presidential candidate in modern times, Hillary Clinton. More than any pollster or political pro, the Trump campaign had one big asset: Donald Trump.

Chapter 10 - THE GROUND GAME

Donald Trump had said that Russia was a natural ally in the war against Muslim radicalism, and this statement was conflated into a scandal that alleges that Trump was colluding with Russia to manipulate the election, a charge that is totally baseless and false.

The bigger scandal was how the Obama administration and the State Department under Hillary Clinton allowed Arab terrorism to spread by looking the other way. ISIS itself had planned to use harmless-looking immigrants to infiltrate the United States to wreak havoc on the country. The anti-terror tactic of vetting Muslims coming in to the United States was slammed by the mainstream media and Democrats as anti-American, racist, and discriminatory.

Aside from policy, the Clinton campaign was wiping the floor with Trump campaign efforts in key states like Florida and Pennsylvania, where there she had a total of 70 campaign offices in those states to Trump's 3. The focus in the campaign seemed to have deserted it from Manafort's lack of leadership. Under Manafort, the campaign had turned into a low-energy effort, and things were going south pretty fast.

It was at this point that Bannon suggested that Trump hired David Bossie as a deputy manager. Bossie was one of the most influential Republican political operatives at the time, who had been president of the 500,000-strong conservative organization, Citizens United. Upon his hiring, Bossie started by establishing the *esprit de corps* that was lost during Manafort's tenure. He also reshuffled the schedules for Trump and Vice-presidential candidate Mike Pence by making sure that they were geographically in sync, to maximize the amount of ground that both men would cover.

He then focused on Florida, which most people had concluded was a win-or-go-home proposition for Trump. He reshuffled resources and hired Susie Wiles, a successful and battle-tested campaign expert in Florida. Despite being initially criticized by Trump for not producing immediate results, Wiles endured and, after hiring more staff to help her, began to turn Trump's Florida fortunes around. After ramping up mailing campaigns, the Florida effort was beginning to get results.

A "secret" meeting between Trump and the Mexican president Nieto, where Trump praised Mexicans for their efforts to help stop drug trafficking and illegal immigration, helped. Things started to turn around after this, and Hillary Clinton's double-digit lead in the polls was down to single digits.

Chapter 11 - DIGITAL MADNESS

The Clinton campaign continued on the tired old tack of adding more regulations to control business, and impose more "taxes on the rich", even while most of her campaign money was coming from corporate American and Wall street. She thought that this message was going to go over well in the blue-collar states like Michigan, Ohio, and Pennsylvania.

Trump, being in the business of business, knew how things were really going in those places. More work was being farmed to foreign countries, and trade agreements like NAFTA were hurting the job situation for American workers. The United States was falling behind through many measurements. It had fallen to 17th place in the "business freedom" measurement, and had the 3rd highest corporate tax rate in the world. To make his case, he had to communicate and learn to connect with America, a considerable task, since he was a white New York billionaire in his late 60's.

To bridge this gap, the campaign first turned to Brad Parscale, who had known the Trumps since 2011. He set up the campaign website overnight for $1,500, and teamed with Jared Kushner to run the campaign's digital operations. It was successful from the get-go as the campaign gained voters and donations through the web.

Kushner joined the Trump campaign in November 2015,

where he immediately taught Trump on the finer points of effective Facebook marketing. Kushner, by this time a millionaire real estate investor, was a master in watching, listening, and learning. Like Trump, he would locate experts on a specific issue, get close to them, and learn as much as he could from them.

Kushner teamed with Parscale and Dan Scavino, the former Trump caddy, to run the digital operations for the campaign. They maximized the tools on Facebook and Twitter, and developed strategies where they could maximize voter sign-ups and donations. After Trump won the nomination and things were beginning to look better, the Republican party began to cooperate. Reince Priebus, who took over the Republican National Committee in 2011, brought the expertise of the RNC into the Trump campaign. Priebus initiated the linkup with the RNC, and brought in Katie Walsh, a RNC operative who had been very successful in raising funds. In her first year, she oversaw the influx of $200 million in a single year, an RNC record. RNC certainly had the infrastructure in place, it was now a matter of figuring out how the legion of loyal supporters, the "Army of Trump" could dovetail with the massive and complex RNC infrastructure. It was now "plug and play" time.

The streamlined campaign, which was spending about half of

what the Clinton campaign was spending, was an efficient one. For every dollar spent on advertising, it got $1.70 in campaign contributions in return. Most campaigns made only 70 cents for each dollar spent. The digital operation was doing its job perfectly.

By the middle of September, the polls had tightened, and in a matter of a couple of months, it was all even, as the Trump campaign had come back all the way from ten points down. Campaign research determined that there were still millions of voters, most of them living in the battleground states, who hadn't yet made up their mind. It was time to go after them and Hillary.

Chapter 12 - THE HIGH ROAD

A billionaire who despised Trump, despite supporting him initially, was Mark Cuban. No one really knows why he had a falling out with Trump, but Trump would later say that Cuban wasn't smart enough to be president. Building up to the first debate in September 2016, Trump did 35 rallies in the month of September alone, while Clinton did 17. He went to enthusiastic rallies and had controversial celebrities like boxing promoter Don King and basketball coach Bobby Knight introduce him in front of overflowing crowds.

Crowd size was helped along by a system called a "crowd-building process", introduced by John Pence, a lawyer who was the vice-presidential candidate's son. When the rental contract for the venue was signed and the advance team had finished booking it, the campaign would create segments by zip codes near where the event was taking place, and create email blasts to inform the people in those segments. Live Facebook ads would then be run on the day of the event. Trump did 276 public events from the convention through November 8th, a punishing average of three events per day.

This backbreaking schedule did not break Trump, however. While Hillary Clinton was filmed collapsing in the arms of secret service agents on September 11th, an episode that she attributed to pneumonia, Trump, despite a diet of fast food and simple carbohydrates, showed no signs of slowing down.

The biggest event in the Trump campaign so far would be the first debate at Hofstra University on September 26th. Even as he blew through sixteen Republican nominees in the pre-convention debates, Hillary Clinton would be another matter. She had much more experience in debating, had a much more experienced team behind him, and no matter what the result was going to be, the mainstream media would probably declare her the winner anyway. Added to this formidable backdrop was the estimated 83 million viewers who were going to watch the debate – a lot of pressure, not only on the presidential debate rookie, Trump, but also on his debate preparation team. However, Trump was unbowed. He was going to be D.J. Trump whenever and wherever he was going to be.

On the campaign trail, Trump had been called all sorts of names by the Clinton campaign: liar, thief, cheat, narcissist, no feelings to those less fortunate, crass, unstable, a misogynist, and a racist. Nevertheless, Trump, leading up to the debate, had taken the high road, choosing not to resort to below-the-belt tactics. However, he is stung when his criticism of Alicia Machado's weight was brought up frequently by the campaign, and then the debate. Machado was a former Miss Universe winner who became a cause célèbre for Trump opponents because her agitating against Trump was a two-fer: She was BOTH a female AND a Latino. It did not help Trump that his microphone was malfunctioning during the debate, distracting him, and taking off his edge at certain moments.

Trump ended the debate by saying that while Clinton had far outspent him, but they were at best, tied at the polls. As expected, the media declared that Clinton won the debate, and rolled out stories that the Trump campaign was in trouble. As it turns out, the problems with Machado and Megyn Kelly were a harbinger of things to come on the subject of women vs. Trump.

Chapter 13 - THE HURRICANE

With barely four weeks left in the campaign, Matthew, a devastating category 4 hurricane was about to hit Florida. Two million people had evacuated their homes to flee from a storm that had already killed nine hundred people in Haiti. Matthew, however, took a turn and barely skirted the Florida coast, and the state averted a major catastrophe. The storm had spared Florida, but a big political hurricane was about to slam the Trump campaign.

Things were looking up in early October despite the mainstream media declaring Clinton the winner of the debate. Trump was polling more favorably, and his public appearances were increasingly indicating that he was gaining a connection with the voting public that few in the media knew about, or expected. Everyone in the Trump campaign was feeling good, a sure sign to campaign veterans, that things were about to go south in a hurry.

On the afternoon of Friday, October 7th, Dave Bossie received a text that a *Washington Post* reporter was requesting a statement from the Trump campaign about a transcript that had run on the television gossip show *Access Hollywood*. The reporter sent an audio file and a copy of the transcript that recorded Trump engaged in locker room talk with some people before a cameo appearance on the TV Soap *Days of Our Lives*. In the tape, Trump had made lewd comments about women. It was recorded in 2005.

The tape hurt even when the evangelist Jerry Falwell, Jr. told Lewandowski not to worry, because the country ultimately was not voting for a Sunday school teacher. Trump saw this as a full-frontal assault on him by the Clinton campaign, which also brought up the Machado issue during the debates. Trump could not deny that everything that surfaced about his comments about women were not his, and the effects on the campaign were almost fatal.

Actor Robert de Niro vowed that he was going to punch Trump in the mouth, and Reince Priebus, the RNC chair, seemed like he wanted to take cover. In a tense meeting with all the campaign heads in attendance, Priebus reluctantly told Trump what was in the hearts and minds of most in the Republican establishment: that Trump step aside, and have another nominee take his place, or risk losing in the biggest electoral landslide in history.

Trump did not flinch and told everyone in the room that he was not quitting because he was going to win. After these sobering events, only Rudy Giuliani volunteered to show up for interviews on the five major network and cable shows that weekend. Things were not looking good despite Trump's defiant refusal to pull out. Once again, the mainstream media was writing obituaries for the campaign, and Republican heavyweights like Speaker Paul Ryan wouldn't be caught dead with Trump.

Nevertheless, the born and bred New Yorker was not one to give up. Trump was at this thing until the end.

Chapter 14 - THE RACE TO THE BOTTOM

Donald Trump is the Tom Brady of presidential politics; the best big-game, fourth-quarter player in politics, bar none. Before the second presidential debate in St. Louis on October 9th, the media had already decided that the race was over. In a football game, this would be like the fourth quarter, and Trump was way behind to start it. The pressure that was mounting was crushing as Republican after Republican was urging Trump to withdraw for the "good of the party". The Democrats were rolling out heavyweights like Michelle Obama to deliver the knockout punch. Now, the fourth quarter in this game was about to start, and it started with the October 9th debate.

Trump had a long memory, and the ones from the first debate stung and inflamed him and his campaign to come back in full attack mode. He could not forget the microphone malfunction, but most of all, he wanted to come back against Clinton and all the allegations that were being made against him about his crude treatment of women. While he took the high road in the first debate, this time he was going straight to the bottom.

Assistant campaign manager Dave Bossie was an expert on

Clinton scandals, and no scandals were more distasteful and disgusting than the ones that involved Bill Clinton while he was married to Hillary. For the sake of political expediency, Hillary used a combination of payoffs and threats to make the scandals go away, because staying in marriage while her husband flaunted his unfaithfulness made her look like she was either an accomplice or a helpless victim, neither of which was the right profile for a United States president.

To rattle the Clinton campaign, Trump's campaign rolled out a rogue's gallery of the main players of both Clinton's sexual scandals to attend the debate: there was Kathy Shelton, who was raped as a twelve-year-old by forty-one-year-old Tom Taylor. Appointed as Taylor's attorney, Clinton suggested that Shelton was emotionally unstable, and her allegations could not be taken seriously. Also present was Juanita Broaddrick, who claimed that in 1978, she was raped by Bill Clinton. The third woman that they brought in was Kathleen Willey, who said that she was sexually assaulted by then-President Clinton in the White House. Of course, there was Paula Jones, who the Clintons paid $850,000 to settle a 1994 sexual harassment case as another Bill Clinton sex scandal, the Monica Lewinsky debacle, was unfolding.

The second debate had somewhat of a town hall format where the candidates did not stand behind a podium to take questions from a moderator, but mingled amongst attendees who would ask them questions. The assortment of Clinton scandal personalities infuriated not only the Clinton camp and the mainstream media, but it had the desired effect. It blunted the expected impact of the *Access Hollywood* tapes, and took away any momentum that Hillary Clinton had arising from the tapes.

After the debate, the mainstream media and many conservatives still believed that Trump was headed to a historic loss. The term, "measuring the White House for drapes", must have been the overriding sentiment in the Clinton camp, as most pundits declared that the question was not whether Hillary was going to win, but by how much.

With three weeks to go in the campaign, Kellyanne Conway took Trump to task and told him that his comments about women, especially about Alicia Machado, were hurting his campaign. She said that to criticize things like how much women weighed went to the heart of the struggles of millions of women who struggle and suffer to lose weight. She also told Trump that he had to act like a winner in the coming days because there was no way that he was going to lose.

Chapter 15 - FAKE NEWS

Running against an experienced, formidable opponent is tough enough, but running against a mainstream media that was deadest in wanting you to lose added to the already immense pressure on Trump and his campaign. Fake news not only meant that the media was fabricating or the out-of-proportion blowing up news about Trump, it also meant glossing over, and even ignoring many Hillary Clinton scandals that would otherwise have been huge deals if Trump were involved in them. This included fund raising scandals, deleted e-mails, getting questions in advance during the debates, the Benghazi debacle, the list goes on.

Most people would have withered under the one-sidedness of media coverage, but Donald Trump was not most people. He never backed off from anything no matter how stacked the odds were against him.

Trump had a secret weapon of sorts in the person of Corey Lewandowski. Even if he was fired as campaign manager in July, he continued to have an unofficial role in the Trump campaign doing advance work, and even travelling with the campaign to some events. However, he also had a paid position as a political commentator for CNN, something that many in the mainstream media resented because they believed (correctly) that he was an insider in the Trump campaign.

In the netherworld of media bias, it is okay to have Clinton mouthpieces, former campaign heads, and Clinton apologists like David Axelrod and Paul Begala in CNN, but somehow it is verboten to have a Trump ally as a political commentator. Even if coverage and opining in CNN and the other networks were already overwhelmingly anti-Trump, the media wanted no part of any Trump supporter like Lewandowski.

No matter what his critics said, CNN President Jeff Zucker kept Lewandowski on the payroll because he was good TV, and was good for ratings; in the end, it was all that mattered. Whether it was debating Clinton campaign staff, and even former Trump ghostwriter, and now Trump-basher Tony Schwartz, Lewandowski came across as an articulate messenger for the Trump campaign. Zucker warned Lewandowski not to travel with the Trump campaign to remove all doubt about his objectivity, but he continued to hang around with the Trump campaign, but eventually resigned from CNN.

In the final week of the campaign, the campaign convinced Mrs. Trump, Melania, to have an interview with Anderson

Cooper of CNN. The last week, to the Trump campaign, was do-or-die week, and the Melania Trump interview, together with the last minute FBI report from Director Jim Comey, certainly helped the cause. The Clinton campaign, smelling victory, did not even bother to do polling during the week.

On November 8th, 2016, the greatest game day, the politician won in a stunning upset. Lewandowski called Trump the morning after to congratulate Trump, who told him that he could not have won without Corey. Corey then remembers the four-word reminder that he had put up on a whiteboard in the very first days of the campaign. It was the secret to the campaign's success:

LET TRUMP BE TRUMP.

EPILOGUE - THE TRANSITION

Winning was big, but of course, it was only the start of the Trump era. There was still the matter of bringing a team to the White House for the actual business of the presidency. Everyone had to sober up quickly, and get over the victory hangover. Even as the mainstream media paid a lot of attention to, and applied pressure to the Trump campaign, the media focused on the first days of the selection of the new administration.

Bannon somehow found a copy of the *Romney Readiness Project,* which was a startling revelation to everyone. Mitt Romney was already planning his transition, and looking for people to fill the positions in transition even as he was campaigning for the presidency. Trump had never looked beyond November 8th, 2016, focusing on winning the election.

Bossie would meet some of the candidates at Trump's estate in Mar-a-lago, and he noted with disappointment, that outsiders and even people who had criticized Trump during the campaign found themselves being considered for top jobs in the Trump administration. Reince Priebus, despite coming in late to the team, and was not quite the all-out true believer, though the entire campaign, headed the staffing effort. Trump followed Priebus' recommendation and took in Sean

Spicer and Kate Walsh as presidential spokesman and deputy chief-of-staff, respectively. Spicer and Walsh were also surprise appointees because they had distanced themselves from Trump when things were going south in October.

IN THE OVAL

Trump did not waste any time in acting on his promise to make America great again. When he was giving his inaugural speech, he knew exactly what the state of the nation was, as was going to take steps to improve that state. Among his first moves were to excise the law of the worst effects of Obamacare, such as the tax penalties on people that did not have health insurance.

In his most controversial act, he directed immigration authorities to impose a temporary ban on refugees that were coming from seven nations that were known to be sponsors of Islamic terrorism. While Obama had issued essentially the same orders a few years before, the mainstream media and their surrogates raised a firestorm, once again insinuating that Trump was a racist.

In "lesser" executive orders, he directed federal agencies to promote excellence in historically black universities and colleges, promote the rule of law regarding U.S. waterways, and to restore federalism.

A serious problem arose in the first few days of the Trump presidency – someone, or some people, were leaking information to the press, and Trump was livid. He had had Reince Priebus vet everyone in the White House staff, including Bossie and Lewandowski. Eventually, the president could not trust even his chief of staff, and Reince Preibus was out less than eight months after his initial appointment.

The distrust and suspicions would continue, and Sean Spicer and Katie Walsh soon followed Preibus' exit. Anthony Scaramucci, a former Clinton supporter, was appointed by Trump to head his transition team, and had a permanent position soon after the elections. Scaramucci too, flamed out and left. Even Keith Schiller, Trump's bodyguard and friend for over 30 years, departed.

In the end, the meat grinder that was the U.S. presidency left just a handful of the people who were in the trenches with Trump during the campaign. Lewandowski, who was in a roller coaster of a ride in the campaign, can only proudly say that the he was Trump's campaign manager, and no one could ever top that.

Conclusion

Donald J. Trump draws out the most visceral responses from people. Either you totally love him, or you loathe him with every fiber in your body. There are very few who have no strong opinion about his either way. People who have dealt personally with him have emerged from their contacts with him either one of two ways. They have either been scarred for life, or swear a blood loyalty to The Donald. He is a tough boss, and drives people harder than most.

To be immersed in the crucible of the pressures of a presidential campaign with Trump may be the toughest job in politics, or in any profession, for that matter. The authors, especially Corey Lewandowski, were shoulder to shoulder with the man whose trigger-itchy emotions and decision-making kept them on their toes practically every waking hour, and "every waking hours from their account", seemed like all of their twenty four hours, seven days a week. Donald Trump would be the closest that they would come to working for a deathless vampire – no sleep, no eating, and working and strategizing every waking moment.

But despite the stark portrayal of a man few people really know intimately, the main "character" of the story was the presidential campaign – its intensity, pressure, and the stakes involved not only for the candidates, but especially for the people who toiled in the background, whether brash types like Steve Bannon, or the strong quiet types, like Keith Schiller. The sheer scale of campaign operations – the money involved, the number of moving parts, and the people required speaks volumes about the incalculable desire of the candidates who would dare seek the position; as well as and the motivation, ambition, and even craftiness and cunning of the thousands who sink several months of their lives into the grinder that is a United States presidential campaign.

Most work for the achievement of an ideal – progressiveness, conservatism, values, and whatever the candidates are selling. Half of them walk away in heartbreak after the process, hoping for a brighter day, knowing that another candidate in four years will once again light up their zeal to fight for their vision. For every jackal like a Paul Manafort, there are thousands of true believers like John McEntee, who lived and breathed Republican politics. They are all thrown in a combustible mix that somehow sputters along and delivers when it has to.

The book is, of course, ultimately self-aggrandizing and self-promotional, as the authors continue their careers as professional political consultants. There is also nothing but admiration for their boss, Donald Trump, which is fully expected of a campaign memoir.

Even given all that, the authors still had to deal with a fearsome boss, and a daunting endeavor that required nothing less than 100% effort and commitment. That the two authors were able to stick around for as long as they did is, for lack of a better word, amazing.

FREE BONUSES

P.S. Is it okay if we overdeliver?

Here at Readtrepreneur Publishing, we believe in overdelivering way beyond our reader's expectations. Is it okay if we overdeliver?

Here's the deal, we're going to give you an extremely condensed PDF summary of the book which you've just read and much more…

What's the catch? We need to trust you… You see, we want to overdeliver and in order for us to do that, we've to trust our reader to keep this bonus a secret to themselves? Why? Because we don't want people to be getting our exclusive PDF summaries even without buying our books itself. Unethical, right?

Ok. Are you ready?

Firstly, remember that your book is code: "**READ53**".

Next, visit this link: **http://bit.ly/exclusivepdfs**

Everything else will be self explanatory after you've visited: **http://bit.ly/exclusivepdfs.**

We hope you'll enjoy our free bonuses as much as we enjoyed preparing it for you!

Summary:

Made to Stick

By: Chip Heath & Dan Heath

Proudly Brought to you by:

Text Copyright © Readtrepreneur

Legal & Disclaimer

damages, costs, and expenses, including any legal fees potentially resulting from the application of any of the information provided by this guide. This disclaimer applies to any damages or injury caused by the use and application, whether directly or indirectly, of any advice or information presented, whether for breach of contract, tort, negligence, personal injury, criminal intent, or under any other cause of action.

You agree to accept all risks of using the information presented inside this book. You need to consult a professional medical practitioner in order to ensure you are both able and healthy enough to participate in this program.

Table of Contents

The Book at a Glance

Every one of us has something to share. It may be fact or a life lesson. Whatever it is, you've deemed it important enough to share with the world. The problem, however, is that the world only listens to a select group of people who are able to weave messages that are ingrained in the minds of their audiences. So, how can you make your message "stick?"

Authors Chip and Dan Heath present their solution to this problem by emphasizing the creation of concrete, affective, and story-driven messages through a six-step SUCCES framework presented in this book.

• Simple: Simplifying a message means stripping it down until only the core message is left. What is difficult about stripping down a message to its bare essence is that it also involves the removal of details that are not as important as the core message. To make the core message stick, it should be applicable to daily life. Moreover, you can use "generative analogies" that relate your message to the practical experiences of your audiences.

• Unexpected: By presenting your core message in a new way, you disrupt the "patterns" that form in your audiences' minds, helping them focus on what you have to offer. After forming your core message, you should determine how to make your message stand out. You should then present your core message in a way that breaks from the conventional expectations your audiences may have regarding your message.

• Concrete. Messages stick because they appeal to the five basic human senses — these messages are concrete. Making your ideas concrete is the easiest of the six steps since it only involves associating your message with tangible things — concreteness is what helped Aesop's fables survive the test of time. Making your ideas concrete also prevents you from encountering the "Curse of Knowledge," where you are unable to share all your knowledge with your readers, instead giving them a vague message. Eliminating the Curse of Knowledge will make it easier for your message to "stick."

• Credible. Experts aren't always available to lend a helping hand when needed, so it is important that you establish your own credibility when presenting your message. There are five ways to gain credibility: first (and most commonly used), the use of an antiauthority who speaks on your behalf as an expert in the field your message tackles; second, a detailed knowledge about your topic, as people tend to believe more those who are well-informed; third, the inclusion of helpful statistics that strengthen your message; fourth, the passage of the Sinatra Test that recognizes you have enough experience to be an authority in your field; and fifth, the ability of your message to be tested by your audience for credibility (like the products advertised by Wendy's).

• Emotional. A great way to make your message stick is by including emotional appeal that can induce a stronger response; experiments show that people voluntarily donate more when their emotions are triggered. There are three ways to do this: first, by associating your message with something in which your audience is emotionally invested; second, by emphasizing how your message will benefit audience members by appealing to their self-interests, and finally, by emotionally appealing to the identities of your audience members.

• Story. Telling stories is considered the best way to make your message memorable. It is also the most effective method for eliminating the Curse of Knowledge. There are three very effective plot structures you can use: the challenge plot (overcoming obstacles), the connection plot (building bridges), and the creativity plot (discovering new things).

By implementing these steps, the authors conclude that a message can be remembered and appreciated by audiences for a very long time.

FREE BONUSES

<u>P.S. Is it okay if we overdeliver?</u>

Here at Readtrepreneur Publishing, we believe in overdelivering way beyond our reader's expectations. Is it okay if we overdeliver?

Here's the deal, we're going to give you an extremely condensed PDF summary of the book which you've just read and much more...

What's the catch? We need to trust you... You see, we want to overdeliver and in order for us to do that, we've to trust our reader to keep this bonus a secret to themselves? Why? Because we don't want people to be getting our exclusive PDF summaries even without buying our books itself. Unethical, right?

Ok. Are you ready?

Firstly, remember that your book is code: "**READ54**".

Next, visit this link: **<u>http://bit.ly/exclusivepdfs</u>**

Everything else will be self explanatory after you've visited: **<u>http://bit.ly/exclusivepdfs</u>**.

We hope you'll enjoy our free bonuses as much as we enjoyed preparing it for you!

Introduction

The book begins with an introduction to how certain stories tend to "stick" in our minds for some reason. Two ideas are juxtaposed: the kidney theft urban legend and a random quotation.

The introduction starts by describing the kidney theft urban legend: you're at a bar and a lady asks you if she can buy you a drink. You feel flattered and agree. The woman returns, handing you a drink, and you take a sip. At this point, you lose consciousness. You wake up in an ice-filled bathtub. After panicking for a moment, you notice a note instructing you to call 911. You do this, and the operator seems to be familiar with your situation because she asks you to confirm if there's a tube coming out from your lower back. She then informs you that your kidney has been illegally harvested.

This is an example of a classic urban legend that has been circulated for years. Which raises some important points. You have probably heard this story before — some facts may have been changed, but the basic details (the drink, the bathtub, and the stolen kidney) are all there. Second, it's told as the experience of "a friend of a friend," which suggests that it's an urban legend. Nevertheless, it's the kind of story that "sticks," something we remember even after hearing it only once.

This story is then contrasted with a random passage from a non-profit organization's paper that begins with "Comprehensive community building naturally lends itself to a return-on-investment rationale that can be modeled, drawing on existing practice," before going arguing that "[a] factor constraining the flow of resources to CCIs is that funders must often resort to targeting or categorical requirements in grant making to ensure accountability." It seems obvious that anybody would find it much easier to remember the urban legend than this excerpt. This comparison raises an interesting question: are ideas *born* interesting, or are they *made* interesting?

The introduction now turns to Art Silverman, a worker at the Center for Science in the Public Interest (CSPI), a non-profit organization that teaches people about health and nutrition. Silverman found that popcorn is an unhealthy snack that contains 37 grams of saturated fat per serving, an amount much higher than the recommended daily intake. The problem that Silverman now faces is how to communicate this information so that others can remember. Truth be told, "Popcorn contains 37 grams of saturated fat" isn't a catchy phrase and appeals to almost no one.

Silverman's solution was to "re-brand" the information and present it with visuals. The plan worked — the CSPI called a press conference, advertising a medium-sized popcorn in a typical movie theater as being more "artery-clogging" than "a bacon-and-eggs breakfast, a Big Mac and fries for lunch, and a steak dinner with all the trimmings— combined!" Along with this message, the CSPI also provided visual cues by juxtaposing these foods in front of the press.

The story was immediately picked up by top news channels in the United States, making newspaper headlines. Even members of the entertainment industry commented on and joked about the news.

This eventually resulted in people boycotting popcorn until its manufacturers removed the "bad" oil, forcing popcorn manufacturers to stop using coconut oil in their products.

This story teaches that a fact can be presented to be just as popular as an urban legend. The workers at CSPI knew that they had vital information that they should share with everyone, and they thought of an effective way to do so.

Let's examine the story and compare it to the urban legend. Of course, the popcorn story pales in comparison to the urban legend. There were no games of deceit, no bathtubs, and no theft involved. It was all about the fact that popcorn is unhealthy. In fact, the information is boring when examined in its bare essentials. The popcorn story is just like any other piece of information out there — it's boring, it's not interesting, it's not sensational, but it is *vital*.

People struggle to make ideas sound interesting, which brings us to the focal point of the book. The book is touted as a manual anybody can use to make their stories or speeches interesting enough to captivate and motivate audiences.

You may also need to consider why you want to make your ideas interesting. Out of all the possible things you can say, why should *this* particular fact be something that *should* be shared to the general public? This is the first question that needs to be answered to set your goal.

In addition, you should also be concerned about your target audience, as this will determine the success of your idea. What does your audience care about? What captures their attention?

The main problem with advertising messages and making those messages "stick" in the minds of your audience members is called the "Curse of Knowledge." Even though the presenter has a lot of insider information, much of this information is unknown to the audience. This can be illustrated by the game of tappers and listeners, wherein a person would try to "tap" a tune and have listeners guess the name of the tune being tapped. To the tapper, the game is quite easy, as he or she knows the song. However, the listener doesn't have this information, and has to guess the song based on the rhythm being tapped.

Based on their experiences, the authors have determined that there are six principles at play when creating a message that "sticks" in people's minds. These six principles will be discussed in detail throughout the course of the book.

Simplicity: The objective is to strip down your idea to its bare essentials. The problem here doesn't lie in removing unimportant parts of the message — the hardest thing to do is removing important information that is *not* essential. Therefore, the goal is to prioritize information. Which aspects of the message are absolutely necessary? Which are useful to the audience but not really important for them to know?

Unexpectedness: This idea has to do with capturing the attention of your audience. Rather, how can one maintain the eagerness of audience members to hear and share the information you impart to them? The best way to capture the attention of your audience members is to completely shake their expectations. Surprise and a continuous generation of curiosity and interest can help you engage your readers in a continuous discussion.

Concreteness: According to the authors, this is the easiest concept to implement and accept. An idea is considered to be "concrete" (and easy to remember) if it can be detected by our basic senses. This shows that the "Curse of Knowledge" is the worst enemy of an effective advertisement, since the former promotes the opposite of a concrete message.

Credibility: This factor focuses on the believability of the idea. As a person with an important message, how will you ensure that people believe what you have to say? A surgeon's ideas on medicine and medical technology will be easily accepted as fact. However, such an authority is not always readily available; doctors aren't always on call to verify the effectiveness of a particular medical product.

Emotions: Apart from showing concrete and simple facts to the audience, you also need to touch their hearts. Ideas need to have an affective aspect for them to "stick" in people's minds, as statistics and facts in and of themselves do not evoke emotion in people. Humans naturally gravitate to something concrete; they need to develop emotions towards a certain message for that message to be impactful.

Stories: Finally, a message should tell a story that encourages people to act on the ideas you share. Firefighters talk about their experiences with one another, helping each other develop job skills and knowledge that could come in handy in the future. In the same vein, hearing stories helps people respond to situations quicker and easier.

The authors explain that a person does not need to be a master advertiser to implement these principles. One simply needs to be compassionate and wise enough to understand what kind of information to share with others and how.

Chapter One: Simple

One of the most significant things you need to understand in order to make your message "stick" is to make your message as simple as possible.

The objective is to simplify your message by stripping it down to its core essentials. Weeding out unimportant ideas is the easy part. What's difficult is determining which of the remaining important ideas are *the most important.*

An example of finding the core message the Army's use of a Commander's Intent. The Commander's Intent, or CI, is a simple order given to military personnel that encapsulates both its goal and desired outcome. It is specific enough to be understood by its target audience but not too detailed to reveal any secrets. For instance, the CI might say "take the bridge" instead of providing instructions on how to take the bridge.

Like journalists, you should develop your message based on the "inverted pyramid" structure. The most important information is put on top of the pyramid and shared first with the audience, which is then followed by the second most important piece of information, and so forth, until the least important information is shared. This method is great since the message is directly expressed upon first contact. However, the issue with the inverted pyramid structure stems from the difficulties journalists experience in finding their core messages — what the readers really care about.

Any issues with finding the core and developing an effective lead can be resolved with the help of "forced prioritization." This means that as the writer, you need to force yourself to determine the most important information to be shared to the public. Say that you only have one shot at sharing the information you know — what would be the one sentence that entails everything you wish to say?

The problem with forced prioritization is that it can be very difficult, since one needs to remove all the important details except for those you are including in your core message.

You may think that it's not that big of a deal. From an outside perspective, it's easy to judge people for making wrong decisions when determining which idea is most important. However, step into their shoes and you'll realize that prioritization is more than just making a choice. This is because a message that "sticks" should include, above everything else, information that is "critical", followed by information that is "beneficial".

Distinguishing between what is critical and beneficial information can be a daunting task, especially since information can be *both* critical *and* beneficial.

This problem with choosing the most essential information can often lead to "decision paralysis", wherein you lose your actual ability to make a decision.

"Sharing the core" means using it to engage the audience in discussion. To motivate your audience members, you can let them apply your core message to make decisions.

The most significant part of this approach is to make your core profound and compact. That way, your message can imply a sense of urgency and worth that tells your audience to apply it in their lives.

A good way to create a profound and compact core is by pitching schema to your audience, which can be done by utilizing "generative analogy," an organizational framework that helps with idea creation. Generative analogy is especially prevalent in Hollywood; to obtain approval from studios to produce films, movie producers need to present "high concept pitches" that are essentially "core proverbs" in the form of analogies that help studios understand what the movie is about while also eliciting excitement.

For instance, the movie "Speed" was originally pitched as "*Die Hard* on a bus, while *Alien* was pitched as "Jaws on a spaceship." Moreover, *E.T.* was pitched as ""Lost alien befriends lonely boy to get home" while *Going on 30* was advertised as "*Big* for girls." What these phrases have in common is that they reference past movies and use simple words in order to explain the storyline of an entire movie.

Chapter Two: Unexpected

Now that you know how to create and identify your core message, the next thing that you should do is to get it across to your audience. One of the most important keys for effective communication is to capture the attention of your audience. You may not think that this is difficult, but given the fact that your message should "stick" in the minds of your readers long enough for them to understand and appreciate your message, it actually takes some work.

For example, consider how flight attendants give safety instructions to passengers. People don't usually pay attention to them (particularly those who fly all the time) because the safety instructions are all the same among regardless of which airline you're flying. This says a lot about your current predicament: important information is ignored because it is not conveyed in a manner that captures the attention of your audience. Although you can demand attention in certain occasions, many times you can't. What needs to happen is that you need to *attract* people so they want to listen to what you have to say.

The best way to be noticed is by bringing people something they don't expect. People tend to form patterns that help them to make sense of the world around them. If you manage to *break* these patterns, you create chaos and effectively gain the attention of your audience long enough for them to focus on you and your message.

However, note that humans can easily adapt to new patterns. Biologically, we find it easy to get used to continuous sensory stimulation, such as traffic noise, the hum of air conditioners, or the sight of something familiar (like a bookshelf in your home). People only become conscious of something if it is out of the ordinary. For example, if the air conditioner suddenly breaks down, it will catch your attention.

Apart from being able to adapt to new patterns, our brains are also wired to easily detect changes. Changes help capture the attention of humans. This chapter focuses on how to capture and maintain people's attention.

To do so, you must first understand two very important emotions: surprise and interest.

Surprise captures people's attention; surprising facts can easily captivate an audience. On the other hand, interest maintains people's attention. Different kinds of surprising things can continue to be interesting because they make the audience curious for more information. For instance, conspiracy theories continue to capture people's interest because new information and gossip about a particular topic is always being made available to fuel this obsession. For your message to "stick," it must be both surprising and interesting.

An issue with making things surprising is that gimmickry is difficult to avoid. It can be very easy to fill your message with gimmicks just to get the attention of your readers. Focusing too much on surprising people with gimmicks can take you off course, leading to a surprising yet confusing advertisement, rendering the element of surprise useless.

The best process to make ideas stick with your audience members includes the following steps:

- Determine your central message by looking for the "core." As discussed in the previous chapter, you need to determine what it is exactly that you want your audience to know.

- Understand what makes your message special. What information has the best chance of surprising your audience? Prioritize the most important piece of information and use that as a way to lure your audiences into discussion.

- Communicate your core message by surprising your audience. Do this in a way that will prevent them from relying on conventional guesswork, only for you to help refine it so they can understand your message.

- Add mystery stories to make your message surprising and interesting to your audience. Stories are a huge part of surprising people, as they do the exact opposite of informing — they keep audiences on edge, leading members to ask questions while keeping them on their toes.

- Open gaps in your message and then then gradually close those gaps. Studies have shown that audiences are smart enough to fill in the holes themselves. Therefore, it's your job to design your statements so that they first provide facts while withholding vital information that will not be easily guessed by your audiences before your big reveal. These "knowledge gaps" can help capture the interest of your audiences because the unresolved story has an air of mystery. Knowledge gaps pique your audience's curiosity to find out more about your message.

News reporters usually make ideas stick with their audiences by providing statements such as "a new drug is sweeping teenage communities today, and you may have it in your medicine cabinet. Stay tuned for more details." These statements sticks with audiences by creating insight and encouraging audiences to ask questions and expect answers. However, audiences are not entirely left in the dark because they are provided with some facts; all they need is a few more details to piece the story together, which you will provide.

In conclusion, you need to find a way to make your core message unexpected for it to "stick" in the minds of your audiences. To do this, you must design your statement so that it interests your readers while leaving gaps to prolong their interest until you fill in those gaps. This way, you will encourage your audiences to communicate with you, making it easier for you to get your message across.

Chapter Three: Concrete

Another important factor that must be considered when creating a message that "sticks" is concreteness. Of the six things that you need to consider in order to create a sticking message, this is the easiest to implement and put into action. The reason why it is the easiest is because people natural gravitate towards tangible things.

Consider Aesop's fables, which have been famous for the past 2,500 years. Stories such as "The Boy Who Cried Wolf," "The Wolf in Sheep's Clothing," and "The Fox and the Grapes" are consistently popular throughout the centuries as examples of concreteness. These stories are considered concrete because they give readers a solid story that communicate a specific lesson. Now, compare the story of the fox and the grapes to a saying such as "don't be a jerk when you fail." Which one do you think will be remembered by generations to come? The story will undoubtedly be much more memorable for audiences, as the latter statement provided does not have staying power; it isn't memorable, just a fact.

Something is considered to be concrete when it can be detected by our basic senses. One of the best examples of applying concreteness is the mathematical education of children in Asian countries. Asian-educated children are generally more capable of solving mathematical problems compared to their American counterparts.

Many Americans assume that this is because Asian children are taught mathematics through rote memorization and rigid structures, but this is far from the truth. Researchers observed that some Asian math teachers would associate abstract numbers with real-life objects such as sticks and boxes to teach mathematical concepts such as subtraction. Not only did they learn mathematics with physical objects, but students also understood the concept of subtraction because they were physically "taking away" objects from a set of objects. An abstract idea such as mathematics was made concrete, making it much easier to learn.

This fact can also be applied in everyday situations. If you've ever read an academic paper, you may have been confused by unfamiliar terms in some works. Since you didn't understand the words, you may have wished that the authors could have provided examples to illustrate their points. Furthermore, when it comes to cooking, abstract instructions also don't make sense; "Cook until the mix reaches a hearty consistency" is much more difficult to understand than being told how many minutes to cook the mix or being shown an image of what a hearty consistency should look like.

When creating a message that sticks, concreteness should be prioritized. Human memory is designed to remember concrete words such as "avocado" or "bicycle" much more easily than abstract concepts like "personality" or "justice."

Other experiments have demonstrated the human need for concrete ideas. For instance, Jane Elliott, a third-grade teacher from Iowa, was faced with the difficult task of explaining racism to her students so they could understand why someone would want Martin Luther King Jr. dead. She devised a plan in which she divided the class between brown eyed and blue-eyed students, with the brown-eyed students being treated as the "superior" group, getting perks that the blue-eyed students didn't get. This experiment resulted in the brown-eyed children feeling innately better than the blue-eyed children. On the other hand, the blue-eyed children felt that they were inferior to their brown-eyed counterparts. This illustration of racism resonated so strongly with her students that they still remember her classroom experiment fifteen years later on a television show. What this proves is that abstract concepts such as racism can be easily absorbed into the long-term memory if developed using concrete ideas.

Going back to the kidney theft urban legend that was discussed in the introduction, you will realize that this story sticks because of its many uses of concrete images. Notice that the basic "facts" of the story (the drink, the bathtub, and the missing kidney) are very notable, making the story memorable as a whole. Not to mention that there is a lot of available information about illegal kidney transplants.

The kidney theft story illustrates a significant point regarding the biggest enemy of concreteness called the "Curse of Knowledge." The difference between a novice and an expert is that an expert can view things abstractly, while a novice only requires concrete evidence. This is true when contrasting a jury and a judge, wherein a jury relies on concrete images presented to them like people's clothing, mannerisms, and actions in the courtroom. On the other hand, the judge views these cases differently based on past experiences. As you can imagine, different views can result in different opinions even on the same case. The goal for you, therefore, is to speak in a language that everyone can understand regardless of their schema. This universal language will be the concrete concept you will use to get people to understand what you have to say.

Chapter Four: Credible

After concreteness comes credibility; you need your audience to trust what you're saying, and one way to gain people's trust is by establishing yourself as an authority in your field. We tend to base our beliefs on those of authorities, or anyone with enough skills or experiences. If we need to prove something, a professional can sometimes come in and verify things. However, this is not always possible. Therefore, how do *you* turn yourself into a figure of authority? This chapter deals with how you can make yourself an authority figure in your field.

There are five ways for you to become an authority: use an anti-authority, use concrete information, use statistics, use the Sinatra test, and use credentials that can be tested.

- Using an anti-authority: Imagine a scientist reporting that a particular bacterium causes ulcers. However, people don't believe him because they didn't understand the evidence he presented to support his statement. To prove his hypothesis, the doctor swallows the bacteria. He obviously developed ulcers, thus proving his statement and making himself an authority figure. Of course, you shouldn't have to swallow anything dangerous for you to make yourself an authority figure. An anti-authority can be used to demonstrate a point. A dying smoker can show the dangers of smoking, making that dying smoker an example of an anti-authority. Furthermore, a non-profit organization that claims to be helping homeless people find employment can send cars to pick up their clients, only for them to find out that the drivers are former homeless people.

- Using details: It's not always possible to get an anti-authority to vouch for your message. Therefore, as a speaker, you need to have "internal credibility." You need to be believed as an authority without needing to outsource credibility to anyone else. You can do this by having a deep knowledge of important details about your topic. For instance, custody was granted by a jury in a case where a lot of evidence was provided, regardless of how irrelevant the information is, compared to the provision of a few yet important details. Urban legends such as the kidney theft story and others also demonstrate that the staying power and authority of stories and people can come from their use of vivid details.

- Using statistics. Although this has countlessly been proven to be an effective course of action, it is still important to bear in mind that statistics need to be used correctly to work. Statistics don't have inherent meaningfulness — they are just numbers. Their ultimate purpose should be to show a relationship (or lack thereof) between two elements. It is much more important for your audience to remember *the relationship* rather than *the number*. Use the statistics as input, not as output; the statistics should be there to support your point, not the other way around. You can also ensure that your statistics are effective by making them more relatable; for example, you can use analogies and concrete examples that are easily understandable to your audience.

- Using the Sinatra Test: There is a line in Frank Sinatra's song "New York, New York" that should resonate with you: "if I can make it there, I can make it anywhere." In making yourself look credible to your audience, you can use the same mantra. An example is considered to have passed the Sinatra test if it alone can establish your credibility. For example, if you have For Knox's security contract, you will find yourself in the running for literally *any* security contract. If you've managed to cater in the White House, you will find it easy to compete for any catering contract. The authors use Safexpress as an example, which is a delivery company in India. Although it is popular with its "on time delivery", it has not yet succeeded in gaining the trust of Indian companies who were dubious of the high rates Safexpress charges. As a result, Safexpress decided to gain the trust of these companies by winning a delivery contract with a major Bollywood studio, a feat which was deemed implausible at the time given the prevalence of piracy in the country. However, since the company had experience in delivering risky materials perfectly — specifically the fifth *Harry Potter* novel which required the same, if not a higher level of security — Safexpress managed to secure the deal.

- Using testable credentials: You can make yourself and your core message even more credible by convincing your audience that they can test the idea for themselves. One of the most important example of this method is the "Where's the Beef" commercial advertised by Wendy's in the 1980s. The ad suggested that the hamburgers served at Wendy's contained more burger than bun compared to burgers from other fast food stores. Wendy's supported this statement by encouraging customers to verify this for themselves. Former U.S. President Ronald Reagan also used this tactic to win the 1980 presidential election when he asked "are you better off than you were four years ago?" during one of the presidential debates.

Making yourself a credible source of information goes beyond just knowing and having facts to support your statements. You need to have personal credibility through your knowledge of important details and experiences so that you are seen as a trustworthy authority by your audience members.

Chapter Five: Emotional

Once you've established your credibility, the next thing you should focus on is the emotional appeal of your message. As mentioned previously, people respond more strongly towards emotional appeals. However, this chapter will not focus on making your audience cry, encourage you to push their emotional buttons. That's actually a bit of an overstep. Rather, this chapter will focus on making people care about your message instead of being apathetic towards it.

In order for people to take action, they must care. The same principle extends to your message — if you want your readers to care about your message, they must be motivated enough by their emotions to do something about it.

To provide an illustration, the authors describe a study that showed the power of emotions to move people. This study was focused on the solicitation of funds for the starving children of Africa. The researchers presented two appeals — a carefully constructed appeal based on statistics and data, and an emotional depiction of one African child. The emotional appeal that used the child earned more donations than the one with the statistics; an interesting aspect of the study revealed that people tend to give more money each time they were presented with the emotional appeal, even if they were also shown statistics and data. However, donations severely decreased when participants were asked to focus on anything related to mathematics at any point during the conversation.

This study greatly demonstrates how humans can be emotionally motivated to act upon a cause while being unmotivated by facts alone. Putting on an "analytical hat" of some sort prevents people from feeling emotions, which in turn prevents them from caring about your message.

Therefore, your goal is to take off the analytical hats of your audience members. The best way to get your message across and acted upon is if you associate it with particular individuals. You can show how your ideas are 1) related to things that your audience cares about, or 2) appealing to their interests while also appealing to their present or even future identities.

The best way to make people care about your cause is to associate your cause with something in which they are emotionally invested. The power of association is an essential tool you can use to communicate your message to your readers.

The issue that you need to face is to find a novel way to associate your message with something your audience cares about. Though necessary, this can be quite difficult, as many words and concepts have been already used that they have lost their appeal, an issue known as "semantic stretch."

For instance, you may hear words or phrases that used to be popular; there are certain words that we deem as "lame" because they no longer appeal to us. Think back to the seventies when people used to say that something they liked was "groovy". Why exactly did this term go out of fashion? Probably because it was overused; the word "groovy" has been associated with being "cool" for so long that it basically stopped being "cool" itself. This has happened very often with many words and phrases, so it's your job to find a new and interesting way to linguistically interest people in your project.

One good example of overcoming a tired phrase is the case of "sportsmanship." This word has lost its value and has become synonymous with "the prize given to the losers of the game." Since the word "sportsmanship" has lost its value, advocates decided that something should be done in order to get that value back. This was done by "rebranding" the word "sportsmanship" as "honoring the game", which gives people the idea that if they care about the sport, they will care about the game.

The same thing can be done with your message. Using the "power of association," how can you make your message stronger? What universally appealing idea can you use to emotionally petition audience members so that they care about your message?

Another idea that could help you get the interest of your readers is appealing to their self-interest. Advertisers can make mistakes by focusing on the features of their products rather than talking about their benefits, as customers can ask "Sure, this product has a lot of features, but how will I personally benefit from this?" Telling people that you offer the "best seeds" is weaker than saying that your seeds will give them "the best lawn in the neighborhood" which is really what your audience cares about.

People do not really talk about self-interest. However, this is one of the strongest appeals you can make that would make your audience care for your message. Advertisers don't talk about selling products by talking about self-interest, yet it's quite obvious that advertisements with the word "people" are more effective than those with the word "you".

When harnessing the self-interest of your members, you need to ask yourself the following questions:

- What will my audiences get from my message?

- How will they benefit from what I have to say?

- How will my core message benefit myself and my audiences?

Finally, you can also appeal to your audience emotions by identifying with them. Your audience don't simply agree to do something *just* because they will get something out of it. In a lot of instances, advertisers think that customers will buy products if the latter are given perks. However, what advertisers fail to realize is that customers make decisions not only based on things that they can touch, but also on their identities; customers often ask themselves who they are, what kind of situations they are in, and what people like them would do in the exact same situation. Intangible things such as a person's sense of duty and self-esteem play a pivotal role in helping people make their decisions.

This idea is demonstrated by a seller who was advertising his safety program to a local fire department. In his training, he was taught the three basic consumer appeals: sex, greed, and fear. He decided to use greed in order to get the fire department to get on board with using his educational films.

The advertiser originally got a resounding "yes" when he called the fire department staff and asked if they'd be willing to view the program he's offering. However, when he asked them whether they'd prefer a popcorn popper or a set of carving knives as a token of appreciation for reviewing the educational materials, the fire department staff took offense; they told the advertiser that they didn't consider to view the education materials just so they could get themselves popcorn poppers.

In the end, the most important thing to remember is that people need to be emotionally invested in your message to believe it. To emotionally appeal to your audience members, you can use three methods: using associations, appealing to members' self-interest, and appealing to members' identities. Regardless of which method you choose to use, the goal remains simple: get your audience to care about your core message.

Chapter Six: Stories

So far, the authors have pointed out very important rules when it comes to making your ideas "stick" in the minds of your audience — be specific with your message and present it in a way that surprises the audience to care about your message. The final thing you need to keep in mind to truly make your message impactful is by telling a story.

Stories are probably the most effective way to get your audience to not only communicate with you, but also to replicate your message in their own conversations. Stories stimulates the mind of audience members by cementing your message in their imagination so that they can remember it days or even weeks later.

In real life, this is always the case. For instance, it is much more effective to train pilots in flight simulators rather than using traditional teaching methods like flash cards or simple discussions. Teachers are encouraged to include the students' experiences in their discussion so that they would be able to remember the lesson much more effectively.

The difficulty in using a story to get a message across is that stories are difficult to create, especially if you're not the creative type. Fabricating stories from thin air may be hard, so an alternative would be to check your environment for available stories. You may not know it, but there many things around you that you can use. Many of the greatest stories ever told were discovered and collected, while only a few fabricated stories have ever stood the test of time.

The authors recount the story of a man named Jared, who lost 245 pounds by eating at a restaurant. Compare the effects of telling this story with that of presenting the company tagline "6 under 7, or six sandwiches with less than seven grams of fat." Between the two, the story is much more effective in inspiring people to eat at that restaurant. The authors also point out how Jared's story matches the criteria discussed by the authors to make a message stick.

- Simple: The core message of the story is simple — eat subs, lose weight.

- Unexpected: The story is about a man who ate himself slim. This story goes against our thoughts of fast food as fattening; since we consider fast food unhealthy, it is much easier to associate fast food with a fat rather than a slim Jared.

- Concrete: There are clear details — oversized pants, girth loss, and the subs. The story is so concrete it almost seems like one of Aesop's fables.

- Credible: The story is credible because it uses an anti-authority — a man who used to wear 60-inch pants has now reduced his weight and is giving us advice on diet and health.

- Emotional: The story focuses on Jared and his struggles. We know that the core message is losing weight, but the fact that the message was told through someone's experiences makes audiences care.

- Story: The story is about a protagonist who triumphs over his struggles; Jared's story inspires us to do the exact same thing.

By this, the authors prove that the best stories are discovered, not created. So, if you want your message to resonate with audiences, you need to find yourself a good story. According to the authors, there are three types of stories that you can consider using:

- Challenge Plot: This type of story would have your audiences rooting for the underdog. This is the rags-to-riches, triumph-over-obstacles kind of story. The key here is for the audience to see the character struggling against and finally overcoming obstacles. Case in point, Jared's inspiring weight loss.

- Connection Plot: This kind of story focuses on people who "build bridges" or develop relationships in spite of great differences. A good story will include friendships that transcend social status, race, religion, or demography. Connection plots are successful because they inspire the audience to connect with the characters. For example, the Mean Joe Greene commercial in the 1970s involved the titular character becoming friends with a small white kid. This kind of story inspires audience members to want to build their own relationships or to be tolerant of others. These stories teach love, compassion, and brotherhood in the face of overwhelming odds.

- Creativity Plot: This type of story focuses on someone solving a long-forgotten puzzle, making a mental breakthrough, or innovatively resolving a crisis. Think Isaac Newton discovering the laws of gravity by observing a falling apple. Such "eureka" moments are characteristic of a creativity plot. Another example is the cases of explorer Ernest Shackleton, who unified his men by keeping the complainers with him while the others were working, therefore minimizing the complainers' influence because they were isolated from the others.

By reviewing these story types, the authors are not intending for you to write your own stories. A story won't help you because you may not be writing or creating an advertisement. Rather, the goal is for you to learn how to spot stories in your environment that you can potentially use to make your core message resonate with your audience.

The use of stories also helps in eliminating the Curse of Knowledge. When stories are told, schema are activated. Stories can remind people of their past experiences, who then use those experiences to help themselves through their present situations.

Stories are great motivators. They are critical in getting your message out there because they actively demand the participation of your audience. Not only that, but they are also concrete, emotional, and are suspenseful. They are everything you need in order to get your message across.

However, the problem you may face is ensuring that your stories are simple enough for everybody to understand and easily remember. When searching for a story, think about what important and concrete details your audience needs to know. You should also think about the impact of your story on your audience.

Epilogue: What Sticks

This final part of the book recaps the main concepts that have been discussed. First, the authors posit the possibility of the audience understanding a different core message than the one you intended. For instance, Sherlock Holmes is remembered by many as having said "Elementary, my dear Watson," but in reality, he never really said those words. Ultimately, the authors judge that your effectiveness in sharing your core message to your readers not only lies in its ability to stick in their minds, but also in its ability to be properly absorbed by your audience.

For your idea to truly "stick," the authors believe that it should make your audience 1) pay attention to it, 2) understand it, 3) agree with it, 4) care for it, and 5) act on it. The framework discussed in the previous chapters simply elaborated on these areas.

It can be very easy to "guess" the effectiveness of the implemented strategies in making your ideas stick. However, it is difficult to verify whether your estimates are right or wrong. Consequently, it all depends on asking the right questions. You should be able to see that your readers can understand and care for your message. Not only that, you need to also be able to touch them with enough emotion so that your message will stick in their minds regardless of the time that passes.

The authors then talk about the strategies you need to take in order to implement the SUCCES framework effectively. The main strategy involves defeating barriers.

The first barrier you need to defeat is the Curse of Knowledge; you must first be able to share a core message that resonates with your readers. Second, you must eliminate decision paralysis by creating a strong message that leads your audience in the intended direction. Third, you need to eliminate the lack of knowledge a lot of your audiences will experience by sharing your core message so it is universally understood. Fourth, you should understand and remember these principles when developing your core message:

- Be concrete. Be specific with your intended message. Let it be simple and strong enough to be understood by a diverse audience.

- Have something unexpected in your message. Go beyond common sense. Make your message stick by telling it in a way that would garner the most attention.

- Tell stories. Attach your message to a good story that would be able to generate buzz. The moral is your message — find a story that fits it. An effective story encourages your readers to act.

With this, the book ends with well wishes from the authors, telling you to "fight sticky ideas with stickier ideas."

Conclusion

The goal of this book is to help you, the reader, find the best way to create a message that has a strong enough impact to "stick" in the minds of your audiences. The authors explain that there is a six-step framework you need to use in order to make this work. Your message needs to be simple, unexpected, concrete, credible, emotional, and story-structured.

• Simple: The most important thing to do in order to make your message stick is to focus on one specific "core message" which you want to share. Stripping down a message to its core means removing both superfluous information and important details. A great way to get core messages to stick is to associate them with the schema (experiences) of your audience by way of "generative analogies." Using these analogies to share your core message will make your idea popular and relatable.

• Unexpected: The goal in presenting your idea unconventionally is to create enough excitement among your audience members to pay attention. Humans tend to form patterns in their minds which assist them in cognition. Breaking of these patterns must happen for your ideas to attract attention. To do this, you must 1) determine your core message, 2) find the counterintuitive concept in your core message, and 3) design a way to present this message in the most surprising way possible without resorting to gimmicks.

• Concrete: The simplest way to make your message "sticky" is to ensure that it is concrete. For a message to be concrete, it must be something that can be understood using the five basic human senses. Stories such as Aesop's fables (particularly the story of the fox and the grapes) have stood the test of time because these fables have concrete elements that make them memorable to readers. Concreteness eliminates any misunderstanding caused by the Curse of Knowledge, and is thus a very important concept in making an effective message.

• Credible: Ethos is another important aspect in making your message "stick." The authors offer five ways in which you can make yourself look credible. First, you can use an anti-authority as an authority figure who shares information relevant to your message. The problem with using an anti-authority is that it's not always possible to get one, so you need to build your own credibility — this is where the other four methods come in. The second way to gain credibility is having knowledge about your message to garner your audience's trust. Third, you can use statistics to support your message. Fourth, you need to pass the Sinatra Test, which means gaining an experience that grants you an unquestioned authority. Finally, you can gain the trust of your audience by having testable credentials. This means that you invite your readers to verify your message for themselves (like what advertisers do with their products).

•   Emotional: An emotional appeal is also necessary in making your message stick. To do this, you can use three forms of emotional appeal. First, you can use the power of association by relating your message to a personal agenda that your audience shares. Second, you can also appeal to people's self-interests by describing how the message benefits them. Finally, you can also appeal to people's identities by clarifying how the message can help them personally.

• Story: The best way to make a message stick is by creating a story. Stories are ideal because they are concrete, have emotional appeal, and may have unexpected twists and turns. There are three popular plot structures you can choose from: the challenge plot, the connection plot, and the creativity plot.

FREE BONUSES

P.S. Is it okay if we overdeliver?

Here at Readtrepreneur Publishing, we believe in overdelivering way beyond our reader's expectations. Is it okay if we overdeliver?

Here's the deal, we're going to give you an extremely condensed PDF summary of the book which you've just read and much more…

What's the catch? We need to trust you… You see, we want to overdeliver and in order for us to do that, we've to trust our reader to keep this bonus a secret to themselves? Why? Because we don't want people to be getting our exclusive PDF summaries even without buying our books itself. Unethical, right?

Ok. Are you ready?

Firstly, remember that your book is code: "**READ54**".

Next, visit this link: **http://bit.ly/exclusivepdfs**

Everything else will be self explanatory after you've visited: **http://bit.ly/exclusivepdfs.**

We hope you'll enjoy our free bonuses as much as we enjoyed preparing it for you!